THESE ARE OUR BODIES

FOR YOUNG ADULT

Church Publishing
NEW YORK

PARTICIPANT BOOK

Scripture quotations from the CEB used with permission. All rights reserved. Common English Bible, Copyright 2011.

Scripture from the *New Revised Standard Version Bible (NRSV)* © 1989 by the Division of Christian Education of the National Council of Churches of Christ in the USA. Used by permission.

A catalog record of this book is available from the Library of Congress.

Church Publishing Incorporated
19 East 34th Street
New York, NY 10016

Cover design by: Jennifer Kopec, 2 Pug Design
Typeset by: Progressive Publishing Services

ISBN-13: 978-0-89869-010-1 (pbk.)

Printed in the United States of America

CONTENTS

INTRODUCTION

Welcome to *These Are Our Bodies: Talking Faith & Sexuality at Church & Home.*

These Are Our Bodies is a Church Publishing initiative designed to encourage conversations among people of faith about human sexuality. Differently aged modules move through seasons of development and connection. Across the program, children will explore how sexuality informs their own identities. Younger teens will look at the larger conversation of sexuality in relationships. Older teens will learn about how their expressions and preferences move them through various groups and communities. Each module focuses on a specific developmental stage of growing up.

But for you, as a young adult, the lens of exploring human sexuality is about as broad as it can be. Simply by virtue of your age, you become world citizens in ways that have higher levels of accountability. There are opportunities and consequences for deeply personal, and broadly global, engagement and activism around issues of sexuality.

This is the *Young Adult Participant Book*. Designed as a companion piece for individuals engaged in a group setting, this small manual provides spaces, prompts, and encouragements for you to outline sessions, take notes, and discover additional resources and reflection around this sacred conversation.

What are the goals?

Our primary goals are twofold. The first is to celebrate and understand the broad spectrum of human sexuality as God-given, and deeply blessed. Second, to build our understanding and embrace of the mosaic of humanity into conversations about how we are called to be healers in the world. As we begin to see one another and ourselves as God's beloved, we are able to make choices about the blessing of sexuality.

In this Young Adult module, our focus is on you—an individual who is interested in exploring both the larger Meta questions about power, sex, life, and communications, as well as the more private intimate questions about covenant, intimacy, courage, and love.

Why are we talking about this now?

We are the body of Christ. Our bodies are sacred ground, and the vessels of our proclamation into the world. They desire, they rest, they play, they hunger. The prescribed avenues for physical satiation have changed so dramatically over the last thirty years that not only do we not know what the church believes about most current issues, we don't even know what society thinks. The moral codes have vanished. More sexual activity takes place outside of the context of marriage than within, and while we do not stand in judgment of that, we must come to terms with what this shift across our culture means for people of faith. Sexual pleasure and experimentation outside of the context of marriage is the norm. Now what?

And even if we, the church, believed that if only people were married, then they could have all of the sex (with each other) they wanted, marriage itself is a moving target. Unions, marriages, blessings, vows, and covenants are racing and back-tracking across local, state, and legal jurisdictions. Some parts of the Anglican Communion will bless a civil union; others will not. Some older couples and young widows, blessed with new lifelong companionship, desire the church's blessing on new relationships but cannot (for many financial reasons) legally remarry, and the church does not have a blessing for them. Many people—because of vows of chastity, the choice to be virgin, physical limitations, asexuality, or singlehood— can each still find pleasure in their bodies. All individuals can still desire to serve God in the fullness of their minds, bodies, and souls.

This program hopes to provide opportunities for conversations that will strengthen your faith while also strengthening your understanding of the role of our bodies, sex, and community through the church and in relationships.

What will we do?

Every session will begin with a reminder of our guidelines for conversation, a prayer, and an opportunity for the facilitator to respond to questions submitted at the end of the prior session. We will then explore the topic of the session through the lens of Scripture, the tradition of the church, and our current experience, through sections called ENGAGE and EDUCATE. Finally, after submitting questions for the following session, we will say our prayers and go in peace.

Where can I find out more?

The *Foundation Book* is the companion text to the entire *These Are Our Bodies* program, including this Young Adult module. You will notice that it is referenced throughout. Grounded in the Episcopal faith tradition, the *Foundation Book* provides theological background and practical guidance about the complexities of sexuality in today's world. It includes essays about the role of sexuality and practical guides to inform church educators, parents, leaders, or anyone who seeks to broaden their knowledge on this subject. Organized into four parts: theological, ethical, biological, and practical, chapters from this resource are commended to you at the end of each session of this Young Adult module.

Welcome to our conversation about human sexuality in the context of our faith. We hope this resource provides a way for you to further explore the complexities of what it means to be human and what it means to be Christian in our complex, ever-expanding world.

—Heidi J. A. Carter & Marcus G. Halley

SESSION 1

THE WORLD YEARNS FOR

ASSURANCE

He made darkness his covering around him, his canopy thick clouds dark with water. —Psalm 18:11

For now we see in a mirror, dimly, but then we will see face to face. Now I know only in part; then I will know fully, even as I have been fully known. —1 Corinthians 13:12

ENTER

To encourage respectful dialogue, growth, honesty, and respect, we invite participants to agree to these guidelines.

I will listen with care to others, and hold the stories and questions raised here in confidence. I will honor the vulnerability in others, and trust that they will honor the same in me.

I recognize that everyone comes to this conversation with different backgrounds, experiences, values, and views. I will respectfully seek clarification with other perspectives to add to my understanding, and if I disagree with someone I will do so carefully and lovingly.

I understand that in order for everyone to participate, I will need to refrain from talking too much, leaving space for others to speak before I speak again.

Opening Prayer

Almighty and everlasting God, you have given to us your servants grace, by the confession of a true faith, to acknowledge the glory of the eternal Trinity, and in the power of your divine Majesty to worship the Unity: Keep us steadfast in this faith and worship, and bring us at last to see you in your one and eternal glory, O Father; who with the Son and the Holy Spirit live and reign, one God, for ever and ever. *Amen*.[1]

---

1   "Collect for Trinity Sunday," Book of Common Prayer, 228.

ENGAGE

This week's topic is ASSURANCE.

There is a mystery to our faith that we value not just as Christians, but as a Church. We do not claim to know all of the answers, and we welcome the questions. As we begin to come together to have conversations, it's important to name, and claim, a space of openness. To embrace both knowing, and not knowing, what a life with God demands.

"This darkness and cloud is always between you and God, no matter what you do and it prevents you from seeing him clearly by the light of understanding in your own reason and from experiencing him in the sweetness of love in your affection. So set yourself to rest in this darkness as long as you can, always crying out after him whom you love. For if you are to experience him or to see him at all, insofar as it is possible here, it must always be in this cloud and in this darkness."[2]

This is not a new concept. As you and fellow group members take turns reading, listen for our encouragement to explore—especially within contradiction—the nature of God in the historical creeds of the church.

"It seems those most likely to miss God's work in the world are those most convinced they know exactly what to look for, the ones who expect God to play by the rules."[3]

....

2   Anonymous, *The Cloud of Unknowing*, ed. Emilie Griffin (San Francisco: HarperSanFrancisco, 1981), 15.

3   Rachel Held Evans, "Dust," in *Searching for Sunday: Loving, Leaving, and Finding the Church* (Nashville: Thomas Nelson, 2015), 109.

The Nicene Creed

We believe in one God,
  the Father, the Almighty,
  maker of heaven and earth,
  of all that is, seen and unseen.

We believe in one Lord, Jesus Christ,
  the only Son of God,
  eternally begotten of the Father,
  God from God, Light from Light,
  true God from true God,
  begotten, not made,
  of one Being with the Father.
  Through him all things were made.
  For us and for our salvation
    he came down from heaven:
  by the power of the Holy Spirit
    he became incarnate from the Virgin Mary,
    and was made man.
  For our sake he was crucified under Pontius Pilate;
    he suffered death and was buried.
    On the third day he rose again
      in accordance with the Scriptures;
    he ascended into heaven
      and is seated at the right hand of the Father.
  He will come again in glory to judge the living and the dead,
  and his kingdom will have no end.

We believe in the Holy Spirit, the Lord, the giver of life,
  who proceeds from the Father and the Son.
  With the Father and the Son he is worshiped and glorified.
  He has spoken through the Prophets.
  We believe in one holy catholic and apostolic Church.
  We acknowledge one baptism for the forgiveness of sins.
  We look for the resurrection of the dead,
    and the life of the world to come. *Amen.*

During the Enlightenment, the Protestant Reformers ". . . shifted their emphasis from the medieval conception of faith as a *fides* (belief that) to *fiducia* (faith in). Thus attitude and commitment of the believer took on more importance. The Reformation brought in its wake a remarkable new focus on the importance of the study of Scripture as a warrant for one's personal beliefs."[4]

EDUCATE

Guiding Scripture

Look at the below verses from Scripture. How do they support or challenge the conversation about faith, trust, and belief so far?

He made darkness his covering around him, his canopy thick clouds dark with water. —Psalm 18:11

For now we see in a mirror, dimly, but then we will see face to face. Now I know only in part; then I will know fully, even as I have been fully known. —1 Corinthians 13:12

....

4   *The Internet Encyclopedia of Philosophy* http://www.iep.utm.edu/faith-re/ (accessed June 2, 2017).

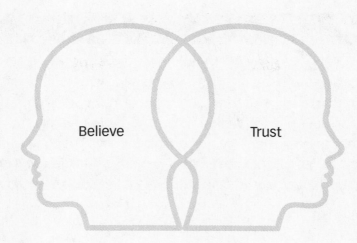

The Question Box

The Question Box (or bag or basket) offers an opportunity for participants to submit questions or comments in an anonymous way. Please take a moment to record any thoughts, questions, or connections that may have occurred to you during this session, or about the larger conversation, on a card. It is our expectation that each participant will drop a card into the container each week, even if it is blank. The leader(s) will do their best to answer each question and share contributed insights at the following session.

EXIT

This session may have stirred in you a new way of perceiving yourself, or others. It might've caused you to reflect on relationships you have had, or hope to have, in a new light. Perhaps you wish to walk or talk differently regarding a new awareness of assumptions or prejudices, and the way society and organized religion treat others. What has changed, and what might challenge your wish to modify your language or actions?

Next Session: The World Yearns for CONNECTION.

In a culture of very public declarations of relationships and break-ups, proposals, pregnancies, where do you see people making true connections? We believe intimacy opens us up to vulnerability, which strengthens connections. Where do you see and experience intimacy with God, the world, and one another, making deep connections? Watch your community, the news, social media, and your relationships for examples of this where intimacy and connection enrich our lives, and come ready to discuss them next time.

For Further Study and Reflection

These Are Our Bodies: Talking Faith and Sexuality at Church & Home: Foundation Book (New York: Church Publishing, 2016), p. 47, Chapter 6: "A New Way of Understanding Our Sexuality."

Closing Prayer

You are invited to offer prayer concerns and thanksgivings. We will share a holy silence before praying together:

Breathe in us, O Holy Spirit,
(silence)
that our thoughts may all be holy.

Act in us, O Holy Spirit,
(silence)
that our work, too, may be holy.

Draw our hearts, O Holy Spirit,
(silence)
that we love only what is holy.

Strengthen us, O Holy Spirit,
(silence)
to defend all that is holy.

Guard me so, O Holy Spirit,
(silence)
that we may always be holy. Amen.

SESSION 2

THE WORLD YEARNS FOR
CONNECTION

My sheep hear my voice. I know them, and they follow me. I give them eternal life, and they will never perish. —John 10:27-28

O God, you are my God; eagerly I seek you; my soul thirsts for you, my flesh faints for you, as in a barren and dry land where there is no water. —Psalm 63:1

ENTER

To encourage respectful dialogue, growth, honesty, and respect, we invite participants to agree to these guidelines.

I will listen with care to others, and hold the stories and questions raised here in confidence. I will honor the vulnerability in others, and trust that they will honor the same in me.

I recognize that everyone comes to this conversation with different backgrounds, experiences, values, and views. I will respectfully seek clarification with other perspectives to add to my understanding, and if I disagree with someone I will do so carefully and lovingly.

I understand that in order for everyone to participate, I will need to refrain from talking too much, leaving space for others to speak before I speak again.

Opening Prayer

Almighty God, you have built your Church upon the foundation of the apostles and prophets, Jesus Christ himself being the chief cornerstone: Grant us so to be joined together in unity of spirit by their teaching, that we may be made a holy temple acceptable to you; through Jesus Christ our Lord, who lives and reigns with you and the Holy Spirit, one God, for ever and ever. *Amen*.[5]

....

5   "Collect for Proper 8" [The Sunday closest to June 29], Book of Common Prayer, 230.

Last Week's Question Box

ENGAGE

This week's topic is CONNECTION.

Last week we asked you to look around your world for places where you see people making true connections. We believe intimacy opens us up to vulnerability, which serves to strengthen connections. Where did you see and experience intimacy with God, the world, and one another?

Guiding Scripture

Listen to this session's Scripture readings for clues about connection.

My sheep hear my voice. I know them, and they follow me. I give them eternal life, and they will never perish. No one will snatch them out of my hand. What my Father has given me is greater than all else, and no one can snatch it out of the Father's hand. The Father and I are one. —John 10:27-30

O God, you are my God, I seek you,
   my soul thirsts for you; my flesh faints for you,
      as in a dry and weary land where there is no water.
So I have looked upon you in the sanctuary,
   beholding your power and glory.
Because your steadfast love is better than life,
   my lips will praise you.
So I will bless you as long as I live;
   I will lift up my hands and call on your name.
My soul is satisfied as with a rich feast,
   and my mouth praises you with joyful lips
when I think of you on my bed,
   and meditate on you in the watches of the night;
For you have been my help,
   and in the shadow of your wings I sing for joy.
My soul clings to you;
   your right hand upholds me. —Psalm 63:1-8

What is the role or purpose of intimacy in relationships?

List acts or gestures that you believe convey intimacy between persons:

EDUCATE

"The story that is the sacred Romance begins not with God alone, the Author at his desk, but God in relationship, intimacy beyond our wildest imagination, heroic intimacy. The Trinity is at the center of the universe; perfect relationship is at the heart of all reality. Think of your best moments of love, friendship, or partnership, the best times with family or friends around the dinner table, your richest conversations, the acts of simple kindness that sometimes seem like the only things that make life worth living. Like the shimmer of sunlight on a lake, these are reflections of the love that flows among the Trinity. We long for intimacy because we are made in the image of perfect intimacy. Still, what we don't have and may never have known is often a more powerful reminder of what ought to be."[6]

....

6   John Eldridge and Brent Curtis. *The Sacred Romance: Drawing Closer to the Heart of God* (Nashville: Thomas Nelson, 2001), 73-74.

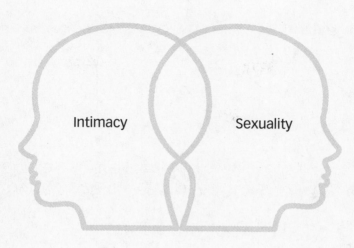

Intimacy   Sexuality

The Question Box: Your Questions

EXIT

This session may have stirred in you a new way of perceiving yourself, or others. It might've caused you to reflect on relationships you have had, or hope to have, in a new light. Perhaps you wish to walk or talk differently regarding a new awareness of assumptions or prejudices, and the way society and organized religion treat others. What has changed, and what might challenge your wish to modify your language or actions?

Next Session: The World Yearns for COVENANT

The divorce rate in the United States has leveled-out, which is partially ascribed to the reality that more and more people have found ways to be in lifelong committed relationships without the added layer of (legal) marriage. Where do you see people, employers, parents, and communities making promises, contracts, agreements of connection, and how do they, or do they, modify the existing arrangements? Watch your community, the news, social media, and your relationships for examples of this and come ready to discuss them next time.

For Further Study and Reflection

Read the section that begins "As social beings, humans are wired for interaction and connection" found on pages 117-118 in *These Are Our Bodies: Foundation Book.*

Closing Prayer

You are invited to offer prayer concerns and thanksgivings. We will share a holy silence before praying together:

Breathe in us, O Holy Spirit,
(silence)
that our thoughts may all be holy.

Act in us, O Holy Spirit,
(silence)
that our work, too, may be holy.

Draw our hearts, O Holy Spirit,
(silence)
that we love only what is holy.

Strengthen us, O Holy Spirit,
(silence)
to defend all that is holy.

Guard me so, O Holy Spirit,
(silence)
that we may always be holy. Amen.

THE WORLD YEARNS FOR

COVENANT IN COMMUNITY

Now the LORD said to Abram, "Go from your country and your kindred and your father's house to the land that I shall show you. I will make you a great nation and I will bless you, and make your name great so that you will be a blessing! I will bless those who bless you, and the one who curses you I will curse; and in you all the families of the earth shall be blessed." —Genesis 12:1-3

ENTER

To encourage respectful dialogue, growth, honesty, and respect, we invite participants to agree to these guidelines.

I will listen with care to others, and hold the stories and questions raised here in confidence. I will honor the vulnerability in others, and trust that they will honor the same in me.

I recognize that everyone comes to this conversation with different backgrounds, experiences, values, and views. I will respectfully seek clarification with other perspectives to add to my understanding, and if I disagree with someone I will do so carefully and lovingly.

I understand that in order for everyone to participate, I will need to refrain from talking too much, leaving space for others to speak before I speak again.

Opening Prayer

Almighty and everlasting God, who in the Paschal mystery established the new covenant of reconciliation: Grant that all who have been reborn into the fellowship of Christ's Body may show forth in their lives what they profess by their faith; through Jesus Christ our Lord, who lives and reigns with you and the Holy Spirit, one God, for ever and ever. *Amen.*[7]

....

7   "Collect for Thursday in Easter Week," Book of Common Prayer, 223.

Last Week's Question Box

ENGAGE

This week's topic is COVENANT IN COMMUNITY.

Typically defined as an agreement or bond, a covenant is usually sealed with some sort of an oath. There are many examples in ancient legal inscriptions and in our inherited texts. Last session you were invited to observe relationships and the world around you to look for agreements of connection or responsibility.

Guiding Scripture

Listen now to the reading from Genesis for clues about covenant, by both what is asked of, and promised to, the parties involved.

Now the LORD said to Abram, "Go from your country and your kindred and your father's house to the land that I shall show you. I will make you a great nation and I will bless you, and make your name great so that you will be a blessing! I will bless those who bless you, and the one who curses you I will curse; and in you all the families of the earth shall be blessed." —Genesis 12:1-3

Promises

Blessings

Covenants

Covenants take many forms in Scripture. They typically, but not always, contain a solemn agreement in which all parties pledge themselves to the others, outlining mutual obligations and responsibilities. Scripture tells about covenants concerning marriage, water rights, tribal relationships, protection, and faithfulness. They include rituals involving animals, exchanges, and other gestures of the now-sealed relationship. In the book of Genesis we find a series of covenants made by God. After making a covenant with Noah (Gen. 6:18) to provide for the protection of his family, and then flooding the earth, God makes a covenant with creation: "I establish my covenant with you, that never again shall all flesh be cut off by the waters of the flood, and never again shall there be a flood to destroy the earth" (Gen 9:9). Covenants are made and held in relationships not only between the individual and God, but within a community also held accountable.

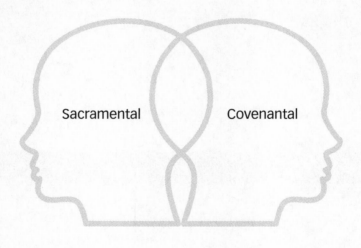

Where have you seen either a sacramental, outward showing of God's grace, or a people or community drawn closer to God, because of a covenant shared?

Are you in any covenants now (either in relationships, with God, your church, or maybe even an organization or community)? Examples: neighborhood, scouting, confirmation, marriage

EDUCATE

In the name of God,
I, *N*., give myself to you, *N*., and take you to myself
I will support and care for you by the grace of God:
in times of sickness, in times of health.
I will hold and cherish you in the love of Christ:
in times of plenty, in times of want.
I will honor and love you with the Spirit's help:
In times of anguish, in times of joy,
forsaking all others, as long as we both shall live.
This is my solemn vow.[8]

....

8   "The Witness and Blessing of a Lifelong Covenant," in *I Will Bless You and You Will Be a Blessing* (New York: Church Publishing, 2015), 152.

This vow and the reading from Genesis suggest that putting words around what is hoped-for creates strengthening and blessing. Do words have power?

Last session we explored the relationship between intimacy and connection. What role does the concept of covenant play in our relationships?

"Five areas of theological consideration in particular have shaped our work: how people are called by God into various kinds of relationship as a *vocation*; how *covenantal relationship* can reflect God's gracious covenant with us in Christ; the ways in which covenantal relationships are lived in *households* of various types; the *fruitfulness* of covenantal relationships lives of service, generosity, and hospitality; and *mutual blessing*, as the God's blessing in covenantal relationship becomes a blessing to the wider community."[9]

....

9   "Handout 1: Theological Reflection on Covenantal Relationship: Spiritual Practice for Gender and Sexual Minority Couples," in *I Will Bless You and You Will Be a Blessing* (New York: Church Publishing, 2015), 127-128.

The Baptismal Covenant[10]

Celebrant   Do you believe in God the Father?

People   I believe in God, the Father almighty,
        creator of heaven and earth.

Celebrant   Do you believe in Jesus Christ, the
        Son of God?

People   I believe in Jesus Christ, his only Son,
        our Lord,
        He was conceived by the power of
            the Holy Spirit and born of the
            Virgin Mary.
        He suffered under Pontius Pilate, was
            crucified, died, and was buried.
        He descended to the dead.
        On the third day he rose again.
        He ascended into heaven,
            and is seated at the right hand
            of the Father.
        He will come again to judge the
            living and the dead.

Celebrant   Do you believe in God the Holy Spirit?

People   I believe in the Holy Spirit,
        the holy catholic Church,
        the communion of saints,
        the forgiveness of sins,
        the resurrection of the body,
        and the life everlasting.

....

10   Book of Common Prayer, 304-305.

Celebrant	Will you continue in the apostles' teaching and fellowship, in the breaking of the bread, and in the prayers?
People	I will, with God's help.
Celebrant	Will you persevere in resisting evil, and, whenever you fall into sin, repent and return to the Lord?
People	I will, with God's help.
Celebrant	Will you proclaim by word and example the Good News of God in Christ?
People	I will, with God's help.
Celebrant	Will you seek and serve Christ in all persons, loving your neighbor as yourself?
People	I will, with God's help.
Celebrant	Will you strive for justice and peace among all people, and respect the dignity of every human being?
People	I will, with God's help.

Do your words and actions matter to God?

The Question Box: Your Questions

EXIT

This session may have stirred in you a new way of perceiving yourself, or others. It might've caused you to reflect on relationships you have had, or hope to have, in a new light. Perhaps you wish to walk or talk differently regarding a new awareness of assumptions or prejudices, and the way society and organized religion treat others. What has changed, and what might challenge your wish to modify your language or actions?

Next Session: The World Yearns for EMPOWERMENT

We have power over our bodies. Other people and systems also have power over our bodies. Through the story of Jesus and the demands of an immigrant woman, we will explore the assertion of power, and the idea of our bodies as currency in our relationships and society. Watch for examples of this, and bring your observations to our next gathering.

For Further Study and Reflection

Read "Sexuality Education for Adults" in Chapter 12, page 95 in *These Are Our Bodies: Foundation Book.*

Closing Prayer

You are invited to offer prayer concerns and thanksgivings. We will share a holy silence before praying together:

Breathe in us, O Holy Spirit,
(silence)
that our thoughts may all be holy.

Act in us, O Holy Spirit,
(silence)
that our work, too, may be holy.

Draw our hearts, O Holy Spirit,
(silence)
that we love only what is holy.

Strengthen us, O Holy Spirit,
(silence)
to defend all that is holy.

Guard me so, O Holy Spirit,
(silence)
that we may always be holy. Amen.

SESSION 4

THE WORLD YEARNS FOR
EMPOWERMENT

Now the woman was a Gentile, of Syrophoenician origin. She begged him to cast the demon out of her daughter. He said to her, "Let the children be fed first, for it is not fair to take the children's food and throw it to the dogs." But she answered him, "Sir, even the dogs under the table eat the children's crumbs." Then he said to her, "For saying that, you may go—the demon has left your daughter." —Mark 7:26-29

Give your hearts, but not into each other's keeping. For only the hand of Life can contain your hearts. And stand together yet not too near together: For the pillars of the temple stand apart, And the oak tree and the cypress grow not in each other's shadow.[11]
—Kahlil Gibran

....

11   Khalil Gibran. "On Marriage," from *The Prophet* (New York: Alfred A. Knopf, 1923), 86.

ENTER

To encourage respectful dialogue, growth, honesty, and respect, we invite participants to agree to these guidelines.

I will listen with care to others, and hold the stories and questions raised here in confidence. I will honor the vulnerability in others, and trust that they will honor the same in me.

I recognize that everyone comes to this conversation with different backgrounds, experiences, values, and views. I will respectfully seek clarification with other perspectives to add to my understanding, and if I disagree with someone I will do so carefully and lovingly.

I understand that in order for everyone to participate, I will need to refrain from talking too much, leaving space for others to speak before I speak again.

Opening Prayer

O God, who before the passion of your only-begotten Son revealed his glory upon the holy mountain: Grant to us that we, beholding by faith the light of his countenance, may be strengthened to bear our cross, and be changed into his likeness from glory to glory; through Jesus Christ our Lord, who lives and reigns with you and the Holy Spirit, one God, for ever and ever. *Amen*.[12]

12 "Collect for the Last Sunday after the Epiphany," Book of Common Prayer, 217.

Last Week's Question Box

ENGAGE

This week's topic is EMPOWERMENT.

We have power over our bodies. Other people and systems also have power over our bodies. Through the story of Jesus and the demands of an immigrant woman, we will explore the assertion of power, and the idea of our bodies as currency in our relationships and society.

Guiding Scripture

Listen as a fellow participant reads the Scripture. Who is involved, and what layers of power, and powerlessness, do they possess?

From there he set out and went away to the region of Tyre. He entered a house and did not want anyone to know he was there. Yet he could not escape notice, but a woman whose little daughter had an unclean spirit immediately heard about him, and she came and bowed down at his feet. Now the woman was a Gentile, of Syrophoenician origin. She begged him to cast the demon out of her daughter. He said to her, "Let the children be fed first, for it is not fair to take the children's food and throw it to the dogs." But she answered him, "Sir, even the dogs under the table eat the children's crumbs." Then he said to her, "For saying that, you may go—the demon has left your daughter." So she went home, found the child lying on the bed, and the demon gone. —Mark 7:24-30

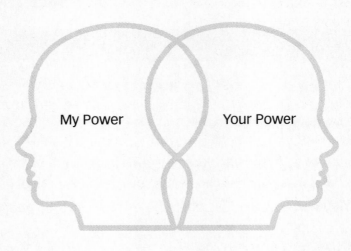

My Power   Your Power

EDUCATE

"In Holy Scripture the man had absolute power over the woman's life and over her body. She existed only for his pleasure and to meet his needs." —The Rt. Rev. John Shelby Spong[13]

Biblical examples of power include patriarchs loaning out their wives for self-preservation, barren women being shamed, and the fact that women were charged with the primary responsibility for all acts of adultery.

In the Scripture reading earlier, the immigrant woman's daughter is healed because she asserted her equality even in the face of Jesus' misuse of power, by placing her body quite literally at his feet. Kahlil Gibran (1883-1931), a Lebanese-American artist, poet, and writer has written:

> You were born together, and together you shall be forevermore.
> You shall be together when the white wings of death scatter your days.
> Ay, you shall be together even in the silent memory of God.
> But let there be spaces in your togetherness,
> And let the winds of the heavens dance between you.
>
> Love one another, but make not a bond of love:
> Let it rather be a moving sea between the shores of your souls.
> Fill each other's cup but drink not from one cup.

....

13 John Shelby Spong. *Living in Sin: A Bishop Rethinks Sexuality* (New York: Harper & Row, 1988), 131.

Give one another of your bread but eat not from the same
loaf.
Sing and dance together and be joyous, but let each one
of you be alone,
Even as the strings of a lute are alone though they quiver
with the same music.

Give your hearts, but not into each other's keeping.
For only the hand of Life can contain your hearts.
And stand together yet not too near together:
For the pillars of the temple stand apart,
And the oak tree and the cypress grow not in each other's
shadow.[14]

How does this poem from "On Marriage" fit into the two-word
diagram about whom has power? Add more notes to the two-
word diagram on page 38 if you choose.

We have used our bodies, and our bodies have been used
by others, across history and today, as currency: as a means
to secure favor or access with God, slaveholders, families; as
currency for fame, cash, and escape; and as currency for social
justice and change. Here are some examples:

- Currency with God, or gods, not just through sacrifice, but
  through fasting, self flagellation
- Currency with slaveholders and sex/child trafficking,
  through buying and selling
- Currency with family lines—through negotiation/
  marriage—for power, access, land

....

14 Gibran, 86.

- Currency—for fame and fortune, through media exploitation
- Currency for cash/employment, as sex workers
- Currency for escape—through drugs, exercise, alcohol, cutting, eating (or not), and sexual addictions
- Currency for social justice—through protest lines, chained to trees and fences, and in hunger strikes

Can you think of others?

How do these situations fit into the two-word diagram about whom has power? Add more notes to the two-word diagram on page 38 if you choose.

The Question Box: Your Questions

EXIT

This session may have stirred in you a new way of perceiving yourself, or others. It might've caused you to reflect on relationships you have had, or hope to have, in a new light. Perhaps you wish to walk or talk differently regarding a new awareness of assumptions or prejudices, and the way society and organized religion treat others. What has changed, and what might challenge your wish to modify your language or actions?

Next Session: The World Yearns for MUTUALITY

We have learned to step away from age and gender-defined roles while exploring concepts of partnership, companionship, and parity in relationships. Watch your community, the news, social media, and your relationships for examples of this where partnership and fairness play an important role in relationships.

For Further Study and Reflection

Read Chapter 8 beginning on page 65, "Responsible Behavior and Decision Making" in *These Are Our Bodies: Foundation Book.*

Closing Prayer

You are invited to offer prayer concerns and thanksgivings. We will share a holy silence before praying together:

Breathe in us, O Holy Spirit,
(silence)
that our thoughts may all be holy.

Act in us, O Holy Spirit,
(silence)
that our work, too, may be holy.

Draw our hearts, O Holy Spirit,
(silence)
that we love only what is holy.

Strengthen us, O Holy Spirit,
(silence)
to defend all that is holy.

Guard me so, O Holy Spirit,
(silence)
that we may always be holy. Amen.

SESSION 5

THE WORLD YEARNS FOR
MUTUALITY

Jesus, being aware that his disciples were complaining about
[a recent teaching] said to them, "Does this offend you? Then
what if you were to see the Son of Man ascending to where he
was before? It is the spirit that gives life; the flesh is useless. The
words that I have spoken to you are spirit and life. But among you
there are some who do not believe." For Jesus knew from the
first who were the ones that did not believe, and who was the
one that would betray him. And he said, "For this reason I have
told you that no one can come to me unless it is granted by the
Father." —John 6:61-65

ENTER

To encourage respectful dialogue, growth, honesty, and respect, we invite participants to agree to these guidelines.

I will listen with care to others, and hold the stories and questions raised here in confidence. I will honor the vulnerability in others, and trust that they will honor the same in me.

I recognize that everyone comes to this conversation with different backgrounds, experiences, values, and views. I will respectfully seek clarification with other perspectives to add to my understanding, and if I disagree with someone I will do so carefully and lovingly.

I understand that in order for everyone to participate, I will need to refrain from talking too much, leaving space for others to speak before I speak again.

Opening Prayer

O God, who wonderfully created, and yet more wonderfully restored, the dignity of human nature: Grant that we may share the divine life of him who humbled himself to share our humanity, your Son Jesus Christ; who lives and reigns with you, in the unity of the Holy Spirit, one God, for ever and ever. *Amen*.[15]

----

15 "Collect for the Second Sunday after Christmas Day," Book of Common Prayer, 214.

Last Week's Question Box

ENGAGE

This week's topic is MUTUALITY, interdependence, and vulnerability.

As a church we are finding the gift of a new path to holiness, primarily in the context of balanced, affirming relationships where the roles of individuals are not gender defined. We are finding new concepts of partnership, companionship, and parity between persons as a critical part of their ability to connect, to trust, to serve and to be served.

Guiding Scripture

As you listen to our session's readings, see if you hear messages that speak to interdependence, partnership, vulnerability and risk.

Jesus, being aware that his disciples were complaining about [a recent teaching] said to them, "Does this offend you? Then what if you were to see the Son of Man ascending to where he was before? It is the spirit that gives life; the flesh is useless. The words that I have spoken to you are spirit and life. But among you there are some who do not believe." For Jesus knew from the first who were the ones that did not believe, and who was the one that would betray him. And he said, "For this reason I have told you that no one can come to me unless it is granted by the Father."

Because of this many of his disciples turned back and no longer went about with him. So Jesus asked the twelve, "Do you also wish to go away?" Simon Peter answered him, "Lord, to whom can we go? You have the words of eternal life. We have come to believe and know that you are the Holy One of God." —John 6:61-69

"And stand together yet not too near together: For the pillars of the temple stand apart, And the oak tree and the cypress grow not in each other's shadow."[16] Gibran

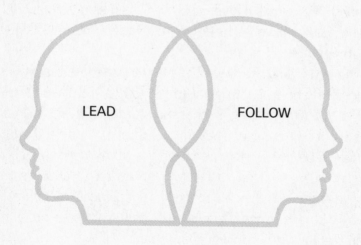

LEAD   FOLLOW

16 Gibran, 86. (See the full excerpt on pages 39-40.)

Barna Group editor-in-chief Roxanne Stone stated that the research shows the collision of new and old attitudes about sex and society today. "The big story here is how little everyone agrees on when it comes to the purpose of sex. This current lack of consensus points to a growing ambiguity and tension over its place in society and in the individual's life." She added, "Sex has become less a function of procreation or an expression of intimacy and more of personal experience. To have sex is increasingly seen as a pleasurable and important element in the journey toward self-fulfillment."[17]

"The Covenant people tend to have a 'we' consciousness. The good of the relationship itself comes first and the needs of the partner are second and the individual needs are third. The covenant only works if each partner, as best as possible, puts the other's needs above his or her own, with the understanding that the other will reciprocate.

The underlying truth of a Covenantal Regime is that you have to close off choice if you want to get to the Promised Land. The people one sees in long, successful marriages have walked the stations of vulnerability. They've overthrown the proud ego and learned to be utterly dependent on the other. They've faced the ways they are difficult to be with and tried to address them. They've gone through all the normal episodes of confession, apology, defensiveness, forgiveness and loving the other most when there's nothing lovely about them."[18]

....

17 *These Are Our Bodies: Foundation Book*, 82.

18 David Brooks. "What Romantic Regime Are You In?" *The New York Times*, The Opinion Pages, March 7, 2017.

EDUCATE

The video you just watched was produced in 2015 by the Police Department in Thames Valley, United Kingdom. They discovered a light-hearted, clear, yet serious way to consider communicating consent in relationships.

There are several scenarios presented. What are both parties communicating in the different settings?

- Coming over often?
- Staying away?
- Trusting the other person?
- Trusting yourself?
- What else did you see?

The Question Box: Your Questions

EXIT

This session may have stirred in you a new way of perceiving yourself, or others. It might've caused you to reflect on relationships you have had, or hope to have, in a new light. Perhaps you wish to walk or talk differently regarding a new awareness of assumptions or prejudices, and the way society and organized religion treat others. What has changed, and what might challenge your wish to modify your language or actions?

Next Session: The World Yearns for RESPECT.

This week we covered the topic of mutuality, and introduced the concept of consent. Next week we will talk about respect and power, and consent and shame.

For Further Study and Reflection

You can read more about the assumptions made about roles in families on page 83 of the *Foundation Book*, starting with "part of the problem . . .".

Closing Prayer

You are invited to offer prayer concerns and thanksgivings. We will share a holy silence before praying together:

Breathe in us, O Holy Spirit,
(silence)
that our thoughts may all be holy.

Act in us, O Holy Spirit,
(silence)
that our work, too, may be holy.

Draw our hearts, O Holy Spirit,
(silence)
that we love only what is holy.

Strengthen us, O Holy Spirit,
(silence)
to defend all that is holy.

Guard me so, O Holy Spirit,
(silence)
that we may always be holy. Amen.

SESSION 6

THE WORLD YEARNS FOR

RESPECT

In the spring of the year, the time when kings go out to battle, David sent Joab with his officers and all Israel with him; they ravaged the Ammonites, and besieged Rabbah. But David remained at Jerusalem. It happened, late one afternoon, when David rose from his couch and was walking about on the roof of the king's house, that he saw from the roof a woman bathing; the woman was very beautiful. David sent someone to inquire about the woman. It was reported, "This is Bathsheba daughter of Eliam, the wife of Uriah the Hittite." So David sent messengers to get her, and she came to him, and he lay with her. (Now she was purifying herself after her period.) Then she returned to her house. The woman conceived; and she sent and told David, "I am pregnant." —2 Samuel 11:1-5

So Tamar took the cakes she had made, and brought them into the chamber to Amnon her brother. But when she brought them near him to eat, he took hold of her, and said to her, "Come, lie with me, my sister." She answered him, "No, my brother, do not force me; for such a thing is not done in Israel; do not do anything so vile! As for me, where could I carry my shame? And as for you, you would be as one of the scoundrels in Israel. Now therefore, I beg you, speak to the king; for he will not withhold me from you." But he would not listen to her; and being stronger than she, he forced her and lay with her. —2 Samuel 13:10-14

ENTER

To encourage respectful dialogue, growth, honesty, and respect, we invite participants to agree to these guidelines.

> I will listen with care to others, and hold the stories and questions raised here in confidence. I will honor the vulnerability in others, and trust that they will honor the same in me.

> I recognize that everyone comes to this conversation with different backgrounds, experiences, values, and views. I will respectfully seek clarification with other perspectives to add to my understanding, and if I disagree with someone I will do so carefully and lovingly.

> I understand that in order for everyone to participate, I will need to refrain from talking too much, leaving space for others to speak before I speak again.

Opening Prayer

> Grant to us, Lord, we pray, the spirit to think and do always those things that are right, that we, who cannot exist without you, may by you be enabled to live according to

your will; through Jesus Christ our Lord, who lives and reigns with you and the Holy Spirit, one God, for ever and ever. *Amen*.[19]

Last Week's Question Box

ENGAGE

This week's topic is RESPECT.

Respect. In session four we discussed empowerment—and the complications about who has, and does not have, power over their bodies. This session will also talk about power, and assess various types of power, consent, and shame.

Guiding Scripture

Listen closely as two fellow participants read the Scripture stories (2 Samuel 11:1-26 and 13:1-22) from the Bible or your handout. Where do you hear allusions to power and powerlessness, boundaries, and consent or lack thereof?

....

19 "Collect for Proper 14, The Sunday closest to August 10," Book of Common Prayer, 232.

EDUCATE

"Power is the individual or collective ability to be or to act in ways that fulfill our potential. Its purpose is to be used for good, but it can be misused to control, dominate, hurt, and oppress others. Most of our religious thought describes power as belonging to God and given to humans as a gift of God. In prayer, many people pray for power as a fulfillment of the will of God."[20]

Power Assessment Activity

What's your score?

Formal Authority	Moral
Expert/Information	Spiritual
Associational (or referent)	Personal
Resource	Social
Sanction	Institutional
Nuisance	Systemic
Habitual	

20 Diversity, Social, and Environmental Ministries Team. *Seeing the Face of God in Each Other: The Antiracism Training Manual of the Episcopal Church* (New York: Mission Department of the Episcopal Church Center, 2011), 23.

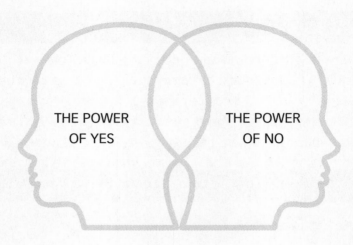

Brené Brown defines shame as ". . . the intensely painful feeling or experience of believing we are flawed and therefore unworthy of acceptance and belonging . . . Shame creates feelings of fear, blame, and disconnection."[21]

- Respect.
- Power.
- Consent.
- Shame.

What was added to these words during your conversations in this group activity?

....

21 Brené Brown, *I Thought it was Just Me (BUT IT ISN'T): Telling the Truth About Perfectionism, Inadequacy, and Power* (New York: Penguin, 2008), 30.

The Question Box: Your Questions

EXIT

This session may have stirred in you a new way of perceiving yourself, or others. It might've caused you to reflect on relationships you have had, or hope to have, in a new light. Perhaps you wish to walk or talk differently regarding a new awareness of assumptions or prejudices, and the way society and organized religion treat others. What has changed, and what might challenge your wish to modify your language or actions?

Next Session: The World Yearns for LOVE

It's a word we throw around a lot, and it is applied to things as small as a song or a favorite food, as broad as sports teams and entertainers, as powerful as God, and as intimate as a child or lover. But what is it, really? Can it be more than one thing? Watch your community, the news, social media, and your relationships for examples of this, and come ready to discuss them next time.

For Further Study and Reflection

One of the easiest ways to show your respect for individuals is to pay attention to the words they use to describe themselves and their relationships, to follow their preferences when in conversation with or about them, and when introducing them to others. In the *These Are Our Bodies: Foundation Book* you will find a glossary, starting on page 221. The language around various experiences and orientations seems to change at a pace that is impossible to capture for long, but understanding the value of doing so is essential, so all you can do is start with today. With the current lexicon. If you have questions, and possibly even updates, on what you find there, feel free to bring them to the next session.

Closing Prayer

You are invited to offer prayer concerns and thanksgivings. We will share a holy silence before praying together:

Breathe in us, O Holy Spirit,
(silence)
that our thoughts may all be holy.

Act in us, O Holy Spirit,
(silence)
that our work, too, may be holy.

Draw our hearts, O Holy Spirit,
(silence)
that we love only what is holy.

Strengthen us, O Holy Spirit,
(silence)
to defend all that is holy.

Guard me so, O Holy Spirit,
(silence)
that we may always be holy. Amen.

SESSION 7

LOVE

Set me as a seal upon your heart,
    as a seal upon your arm;
for love is strong as death,
    passion fierce as the grave.
Its flashes are flashes of fire,
    a raging flame.
Many waters cannot quench love,
    neither can floods drown it.
If one offered for love
    all the wealth of one's house,
      it would be utterly scorned. —Song of Solomon 8:6-7

ENTER

To encourage respectful dialogue, growth, honesty, and respect, we invite participants to agree to these guidelines.

I will listen with care to others, and hold the stories and questions raised here in confidence. I will honor the vulnerability in others, and trust that they will honor the same in me.

I recognize that everyone comes to this conversation with different backgrounds, experiences, values, and views. I will respectfully seek clarification with other perspectives to add to my understanding, and if I disagree with someone I will do so carefully and lovingly.

I understand that in order for everyone to participate, I will need to refrain from talking too much, leaving space for others to speak before I speak again.

Opening Prayer

O Lord, you have taught us that without love whatever we do is worth nothing; Send your Holy Spirit and pour into our hearts your greatest gift, which is love, the true bond of peace and of all virtue, without which whoever lives is accounted dead before you. Grant this for the sake of your only Son Jesus Christ, who lives and reigns with you and the Holy Spirit, one God, now and for ever. *Amen*.[22]

....

22 "Collect for the Seventh Sunday after the Epiphany," Book of Common Prayer, 216.

Last Week's Question Box

ENGAGE

This week's topic is LOVE.

It's a word we throw around a lot, and it is applied to things as small as a song or a favorite food, as broad as sports teams and entertainers, as powerful as God, and as intimate as a child or lover. But what is it, really?

Guiding Scripture

Listen closely as a fellow participant reads the poem from Song of Solomon 8:6-7.

> *Set me as a seal upon your heart,*
> *   as a seal upon your arm;*
> *for love is strong as death,*
> *   passion fierce as the grave.*
> *Its flashes are flashes of fire,*
> *   a raging flame.*
> *Many waters cannot quench love,*
> *   neither can floods drown it.*

If one offered for love
    all the wealth of one's house,
    it would be utterly scorned.

As you are listening, you are invited to make notes on the two-word diagram below.

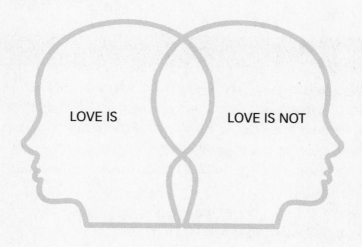

In his book *The Art of Loving,*[23] psychologist Erich Fromm maintains that love is not merely a feeling but is also actions, and that in fact, the "feeling" of love is superficial in comparison to one's commitment to love via a series of loving actions over time. Fromm also described love as a conscious choice that in its early

23 Erich Fromm. *The Art of Loving* (San Francisco: Harper Perennial, 2000).

stages might originate as an involuntary feeling, but which then later no longer depends on those feelings, but rather depends only on conscious commitment.

> "In love there is a feeling of unity, and an active appreciation of the intrinsic worth of the object of love."[24]
> —Spiritual Master Meher Baba

> When reflecting on the story of Jonah, we find that once the beloved is embraced, it is without condition. Those who witnessed Jonah's story "had to see that God's love is unlimited. God's embrace is not restricted by their embrace. God's grace is not circumscribed by their prejudices and by their definitions."
> —The Rt. Rev. John Shelby Spong[25]

As people of faith, how do these definitions of love inform those three opportunities to love?

Love God:

....

24 Meher Baba. *Discourses* (Myrtle Beach, SC: Sheriar Press, 1995), 113.

25 Spong. *Living In Sin*, 37.

Love Our Neighbors:

Love Ourselves:

EDUCATE

Which best matches your experiences of loving others, or of being loved in relationships, and why?

1. "As strong as death . . . a flash of fire . . ." (Song of Solomon)
2. A combination of lust, attraction, and attachment. (brain science)[26]
3. Not merely a feeling, but actions (Fromm)
4. "An active appreciation of the intrinsic worth of the object of love." (Baba)
5. "Unlimited, and not restricted by [being embraced back]." (Spong)

....

26 Defining the Brain Systems of Lust, Romantic Attraction, and Attachment, by Fisher et. al. http://homepage.mac.com/helenfisher/archives_of_sex_beh.pdf

The Question Box: Your Questions

EXIT

This session may have stirred in you a new way of perceiving yourself, or others. It might've caused you to reflect on relationships you have had, or hope to have, in a new light. Perhaps you wish to walk or talk differently regarding a new awareness of assumptions or prejudices, and the way society and organized religion treat others. What has changed, and what might challenge your wish to modify your language or actions?

Next Session: The World Yearns for PLEASURE

Pleasure is both a gift to us, and a moral good, but it can be used for negative or destructive ends. There are seemingly endless ways we pleasure our bodies, including with food, exercise, rest, touch, sex, fasting, extreme sports, and many others. What purpose does it serve? Watch your community, the news, social media, and your relationships for examples of how and where we find physical pleasure, and come ready to discuss them next time.

For Further Study and Reflection

Read *These Are Our Bodies: Foundation Book*, Chapter 3: "The Body As Sacred" starting on page 27.

Closing Prayer

You are invited to offer prayer concerns and thanksgivings. We will share a holy silence before praying together:

Breathe in us, O Holy Spirit,
(silence)
that our thoughts may all be holy.

Act in us, O Holy Spirit,
(silence)
that our work, too, may be holy.

Draw our hearts, O Holy Spirit,
(silence)
that we love only what is holy.

Strengthen us, O Holy Spirit,
(silence)
to defend all that is holy.

Guard me so, O Holy Spirit,
(silence)
that we may always be holy. Amen.

Session 8

PLEASURE

In the beginning was the Word, and the Word was with God, and the Word was God. He was in the beginning with God. All things came into being through him, and without him not one thing came into being. What has come into being in him was life, and the life was the light of all people. —John 1:1-4

Live by the Spirit, I say, and do not gratify the desires of the flesh. —Galatians 5:16

ENTER

To encourage respectful dialogue, growth, honesty, and respect, we invite participants to agree to these guidelines.

I will listen with care to others, and hold the stories and questions raised here in confidence. I will honor the vulnerability in others, and trust that they will honor the same in me.

I recognize that everyone comes to this conversation with different backgrounds, experiences, values, and views. I will respectfully seek clarification with other perspectives to add to my understanding, and if I disagree with someone I will do so carefully and lovingly.

I understand that in order for everyone to participate, I will need to refrain from talking too much, leaving space for others to speak before I speak again.

Opening Prayer

Almighty God, you alone can bring into order the unruly wills and affections of sinners: Grant your people grace to love what you command and desire what you promise; that, among the swift and varied changes of the world, our hearts may surely there be fixed where true joys are to be found; through Jesus Christ our Lord, who lives and reigns with you and the Holy Spirit, one God, now and for ever. *Amen*.[27]

....

27 "Collect for the Fifth Sunday in Lent," Book of Common Prayer, 219.

Last Week's Question Box

ENGAGE

This week's topic is PLEASURE.

Pleasure is both a gift to us, and a moral good, but it can be used for negative or destructive ends.

Guiding Scripture

Listen to the readings for messages about the unity, or connection between the body and soul, and the conflict or disunity between them.

Live by the Spirit, I say, and do not gratify the desires of the flesh. For what the flesh desires is opposed to the Spirit, and what the Spirit desires is opposed to the flesh; for these are opposed to each other, to prevent you from doing what you want. But if you are led by the Spirit, you are not subject to the law. —Galatians 5:16-18

In the beginning was the Word, and the Word was with God, and the Word was God. He was in the beginning with God. All things came into being through him, and without him not one thing came into being. What has come into being in him was life, and the life was the light of all people. The light shines in the darkness, and the darkness did not overcome it. And the Word became flesh and lived among us, and we have seen his glory, the glory as of a father's only son, full of grace and truth. (John testified to him and cried out, "This was he of whom I said, 'He who comes after me ranks ahead of me because he was before me.'") From his fullness we have all received, grace upon grace. The law indeed was given through Moses; grace and truth came through Jesus Christ. No one has ever seen God. It is God the only Son, who is close to the Father's heart, who has made him known. —John 1:1-5, 14-18

As you are listening, you are invited to make notes on the two-word diagram below.

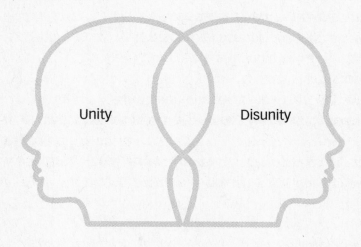

Unity   Disunity

EDUCATE

"[T]he love of self, God, and other are not inherently opposed: we can honor God and honor our bodies by attending to our desires with care; we can help our future partners out by figuring out who we are and what we like and long for. The pursuit of pleasure can be used to mask other needs and, indeed, to debase ourselves. But we need not be afraid to know and love our bodies, for they are gifts from God, made for pleasure, made for connecting us to the world and its people."[28]

Let him kiss me with the kisses of his mouth!
For your love is better than wine,
  your anointing oils are fragrant,
your name is perfume poured out;
  therefore the maidens love you.
Draw me after you, let us make haste.
  The king has brought me into his chambers.
We will exult and rejoice in you;
  we will extol your love more than wine;
  rightly do they love you. —Song of Solomon 1:1-4

What did you hear about pleasure being good for us, and what did you hear about it being a challenge?

....

28 Bromleigh McCleneghan. *Good Christian Sex* (San Francisco: HarperSanFrancisco, 2016), 36-37.

"Our bodies are not base matter to be transcended, their needs ignored or denied in pursuit of holiness. They are us, gifts from God, though, indeed, mutable and mortal, prone to . . . vulnerability and glory."[29]

The Question Box: Your Questions

EXIT

This session may have stirred in you a new way of perceiving yourself, or others. It might've caused you to reflect on relationships you have had, or hope to have, in a new light. Perhaps you wish to walk or talk differently regarding a new awareness of assumptions or prejudices, and the way society and organized religion treat others. What has changed, and what might challenge your wish to modify your language or actions?

....

29 Augustine and Marcus Dods. *The City of God* (New York: Modern Library, 1994), 475.

Next Session: The World Yearns for WHOLENESS

This week we covered the topic of pleasure both for others and ourselves. Next session we will discuss wholeness, and how we might integrate our lives as faithful people in the world, but not of it. Watch for examples of where you might see tension between the sacred and secular, and bring those with you to the next session.

For Further Study and Reflection

Read Chapter 10 of the *These Are Our Bodies: Foundation Book*: "Changes in Culture."

Closing Prayer

You are invited to offer prayer concerns and thanksgivings. We will share a holy silence before praying together:

Breathe in us, O Holy Spirit,
(silence)
that our thoughts may all be holy.

Act in us, O Holy Spirit,
(silence)
that our work, too, may be holy.

Draw our hearts, O Holy Spirit,
(silence)
that we love only what is holy.

Strengthen us, O Holy Spirit,
(silence)
to defend all that is holy.

Guard me so, O Holy Spirit,
(silence)
that we may always be holy. Amen.

SESSION 9

THE WORLD YEARNS FOR WHOLENESS

The eye is the lamp of the body. So, if your eye is healthy, your whole body will be full of light; but if your eye is unhealthy, your whole body will be full of darkness. If then the light in you is darkness, how great is the darkness! —Matthew 6:22-23a

Don't you know that you yourselves are God's temple and that God's Spirit dwells in your midst? If anyone destroys God's temple, God will destroy that person; for God's temple is sacred, and you together are that temple. —1 Corinthians 3:16-17

Therefore, I urge you, brothers and sisters, in view of God's mercy, to offer your bodies as a living sacrifice, holy and pleasing to God—this is your true and proper worship. Do not conform to the pattern of this world, but be transformed by the renewing of your mind. Then you will be able to test and approve what God's will is—his good, pleasing and perfect will. —Romans 12:1-2

ENTER

To encourage respectful dialogue, growth, honesty, and respect, we invite participants to agree to these guidelines.

I will listen with care to others, and hold the stories and questions raised here in confidence. I will honor the vulnerability in others, and trust that they will honor the same in me.

I recognize that everyone comes to this conversation with different backgrounds, experiences, values, and views. I will respectfully seek clarification with other perspectives to add to my understanding, and if I disagree with someone I will do so carefully and lovingly.

I understand that in order for everyone to participate, I will need to refrain from talking too much, leaving space for others to speak before I speak again.

Opening Prayer

O God, who wonderfully created, and yet more wonderfully restored, the dignity of human nature: Grant that we may share the divine life of him who humbled himself to share our humanity, your Son Jesus Christ; who lives and reigns with you, in the unity of the Holy Spirit, one God, for ever and ever. *Amen.*[30]

....

30   "Preface of the Epiphany," Book of Common Prayer, 252.

Last Week's Question Box

ENGAGE

This week's topic is WHOLENESS.

This session focuses on how we might better understand ourselves as both body and soul—integrated beings. We will explore the distinctions, and be reminded that God created and uses both the body and the spirit in sacred acts of loving, liturgy, and remembering.

Guiding Scripture

"...The eye is the lamp of the body," —Matthew 6:22-23

"...Your body is God's temple," —1 Corinthians 3:16-17

"...Offer your bodies as a living sacrifice," —Romans 12:1-2

... [T]hat the Christian religion was the only one that believed God became a human body, and yet we have had such deficient and frankly negative attitudes towards embodiment, the physical world, sexuality, emotions, animals, wonderful physical practices like yoga, and nature itself. We want to do spirituality all in the head. It often seems to me that Western Christianity has been much more formed by Plato (body and soul are at war) than by Jesus (body and soul are already one). For many of us, the body is more repressed and denied than even the mind or the heart. It makes both presence and healing quite difficult, because the body, not our mind, holds our memories.[31]

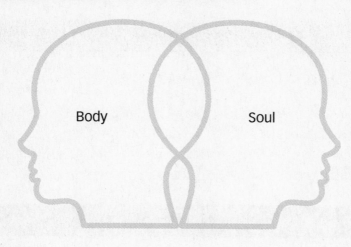

During the discussion, you talked some about the distinction between practices and disciplines that honor and care for our souls, and those that honor and care for our bodies. Is one

31 Richard Rohr's Daily Mediation "How to Stay Open." http://myemail.constantcontact.com/Richard-Rohr-s-Meditation--How-to-Stay-Open.html?soid=1103098668616&aid=jc5Q93T6 Yu8 (Accessed May 27, 2017).

considered better than the other? more self-serving? more God-serving?

Who encourages you to care for your soul? to care for your body? to integrate the two into one whole and balanced being?

EDUCATE

"Scripture looks beyond our sexuality as merely reproductive and places humanity as the object of God's desiring. Sexual metaphors throughout Scripture describe God's relationship to humanity, providing a broader sense of meaning behind desiring. We are relational *and* bodied beings. Our bodies are sexual, and our bodies connect us to each other in collaboration, community, language, culture, and politics."[32]

....

32 Leslie Choplin and Jenny Beaumont. *These Are Our Bodies: Talking Faith & Sexuality at Church & Home Foundation Book* (New York, Church Publishing, 2016), 27.

How *do* our bodies connect us to collaboration, community, language, culture, and politics?

Collaboration

Community

Language

Culture

Politics

"The Table of the Lord . . . The Eucharist . . . is not simply a symbolic expansion of the moral circle. The Lord's Supper becomes a profoundly subversive political event in the lives of participants. The sacrament brings real people—divided in the larger world—into a sweaty, flesh-and-blood embrace where 'there shall be no difference between them and the rest.'"[33]

Where, in your experience, has the Lord's Supper been anything like "a profoundly subversive political event in the lives of participants"? If it hasn't, why not?

----

33 Richard Beck. *Unclean: Mediations on Purity, Hospitality, and Mortality* (Eugene, OR: Wipf and Stock Publishers, 2011), 114.

The Question Box: Your Questions

EXIT

This session may have stirred in you a new way of perceiving yourself, or others. It might've caused you to reflect on relationships you have had, or hope to have, in a new light. Perhaps you wish to walk or talk differently regarding a new awareness of assumptions or prejudices, and the way society and organized religion treat others. What has changed, and what might challenge your wish to modify your language or actions?

This session explored the tension and blessing of living as a unified body and soul. Next session we will explore the mystery of how our bodies are shaped to love and be loved across a number of spectrum of attraction, desire, companionship, and relationships.

For Further Study and Reflection

Read chapter 3, "The Body as Sacred" in *These Are Our Bodies: Foundation Book.*

Closing Prayer

You are invited to offer prayer concerns and thanksgivings. We will share a holy silence before praying together:

Breathe in us, O Holy Spirit,
(silence)
that our thoughts may all be holy.

Act in us, O Holy Spirit,
(silence)
that our work, too, may be holy.

Draw our hearts, O Holy Spirit,
(silence)
that we love only what is holy.

Strengthen us, O Holy Spirit,
(silence)
to defend all that is holy.

Guard me so, O Holy Spirit,
(silence)
that we may always be holy. Amen.

Session 10

THE WORLD YEARNS FOR

MYSTERY

No one has ever seen God; if we love one another, God lives in us, and his love is perfected in us. —1 John 4:2

ENTER

To encourage respectful dialogue, growth, honesty, and respect, we invite participants to agree to these guidelines.

I will listen with care to others, and hold the stories and questions raised here in confidence. I will honor the vulnerability in others, and trust that they will honor the same in me.

I recognize that everyone comes to this conversation with different backgrounds, experiences, values, and views. I will respectfully seek clarification with other perspectives to add to my understanding, and if I disagree with someone I will do so carefully and lovingly.

I understand that in order for everyone to participate, I will need to refrain from talking too much, leaving space for others to speak before I speak again.

Opening Prayer

Almighty and everlasting God, you made the universe with its marvelous order and chaos, its atoms, worlds, and galaxies, and the infinite complexity of living creatures. We give you thanks for all who increase knowledge of and wonder at your works. Grant that as we explore the mysteries of your creation, we may come to know you more truly and serve you more humbly; in the name of Jesus Christ our Risen Savior. *Amen.*[34]

Last Week's Question Box

ENGAGE

This week's topic is MYSTERY.

Mystery is the unknown, vast, and intriguing space where God's nature, creation, and chaos continue to be revealed to us in the diversity that is in one another.

Guiding Scripture

Listen for messages about the biological and gender roles assigned to God in the scripture readings.

....

34 "A Rogation Day Procession and Liturgy," from The Episcopal Ecological Network http://eenonline.org/reflect/liturgy/propers/prayers.htm (Accessed May 27, 2017).

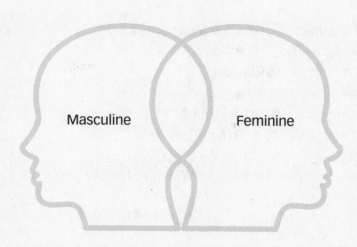

Then God said, "Let us make humankind in our image, according to our likeness; and let them have dominion over the fish of the sea, and over the birds of the air, and over the cattle, and over all the wild animals of the earth, and over every creeping thing that creeps upon the earth. So God created humankind in his image, in the image of God he created them; male and female he created them. —Genesis 1:26-27

"Or what woman having ten silver coins, if she loses one of them, does not light a lamp, sweep the house, and search carefully until she finds it? When she has found it, she calls together her friends and neighbors, saying, 'Rejoice with me, for I have found the coin that I had lost.' Just so, I tell you, there is joy in the presence of the angels of God over one sinner who repents." —Luke 15:8-10

The Lord goes forth like a soldier,
*   like a warrior he stirs up his fury;*
he cries out, he shouts aloud,
*   he shows himself mighty against his foes.*
For a long time I have held my peace,
*   I have kept still and restrained myself;*
now I will cry out like a woman in labor,
*   I will gasp and pant.* —Isaiah 42:13-14

"Jerusalem, Jerusalem, the city that kills the prophets and stones those who are sent to it! How often have I desired to gather your children together as a hen gathers her brood under her wings, and you were not willing!" —Matthew 23:37

EDUCATE

No one has ever seen God; if we love one another, God lives in us, and his love is perfected in us. —1 John 4:12

EXIT

This session may have stirred in you a new way of perceiving yourself, or others. It might've caused you to reflect on relationships you have had, or hope to have, in a new light. Perhaps you wish to walk or talk differently regarding a new awareness of assumptions or prejudices, and the way society and organized religion treat others. What has changed, and what might challenge your wish to modify your language or actions?

For Further Study and Reflection

Many experts in developmental psychology note that stages and changes often flow more like the rings on a tree, where a person moves in and out, often repeating seasons of newness and growth. Many young adults just coming into an awareness of their own identities feel like they are starting over. In the *Foundation Book*, Chapter 13 offers good reminders regarding our struggles for belonging—for safety, affection, and esteem, throughout our lives.

Closing Prayer

You are invited to offer prayer concerns and thanksgivings. We will share a holy silence before praying together:

Breathe in us, O Holy Spirit,
(silence)
that our thoughts may all be holy.

Act in us, O Holy Spirit,
(silence)
that our work, too, may be holy.

Draw our hearts, O Holy Spirit,
(silence)
that we love only what is holy.

Strengthen us, O Holy Spirit,
(silence)
to defend all that is holy.

Guard me so, O Holy Spirit,
(silence)
that we may always be holy. Amen.